A GUIDE TO
STOICISM

By: St. George Stock

This book has been published by:

Contact: sales@ezreads.net

URL: http://www.ezreads.net

Publishing Date: 2010

ISBN# 978-1-61534-203-7

Striving to be a leader in digital publishing. All of our books have been digitalized and reformatted to be *EZ* to *Read* and available in Paperback, two types of Hardcover and several eBook formats.

See our website for a wide range of subjects including most religions, philosophy, historical, classical fiction, freemasonry, esoteric and ancient texts.

Please note that we do not correct out-of-date facts or grammar-type errors that were in the original book. We do our best to retain the original composition of the text, the way the author intended it.

CONTENTS

FOREWORD .... - 7 -

PHILOSOPHY AMONG THE GREEKS AND ROMANS. .... - 9 -

DIVISION OF PHILOSOPHY. .... - 15 -

LOGIC .... - 19 -

ETHIC .... - 29 -

PHYSIC .... - 47 -

CONCLUSION .... - 57 -

FOREWORD

If you strip Stoicism of its paradoxes and its wilful misuse of language, what is left is simply the moral philosophy of Socrates, Plato and Aristotle, dashed with the physics of Heraclitus. Stoicism was not so much a new doctrine as the form under which the old Greek philosophy finally presented itself to the world at large. It owed its popularity in some measure to its extravagance. A great deal might be said about Stoicism as a religion and about the part it played in the formation of Christianity but these subjects were excluded by the plan of this volume which was to present a sketch of the Stoic doctrine based on the original authorities.

PHILOSOPHY AMONG THE GREEKS AND ROMANS.

Among the Greeks and Romans of the classical age philosophy occupied the place taken by religion among ourselves. Their appeal was to reason not to revelation. To what, asks Cicero in his Offices, are we to look for training in virtue, if not to philosophy? Now, if truth is believed to rest upon authority it is natural that it should be impressed upon the mind from the earliest age, since the essential thing is that it should be believed, but a truth which makes its appeal to reason must be content to wait till reason is developed. We are born into the Eastern, Western or Anglican communion or some other denomination, but it was of his own free choice that the serious minded young Greek or Roman embraced the tenets of one of the great sects which divided the world of philosophy. The motive which led him to do so in the first instance may have been merely the influence of a friend or a discourse from some eloquent speaker, but the choice once made was his own choice, and he adhered to it as such. Conversions from one sect to another were of quite rare occurrence. A certain Dionysius of Heraclea, who went over from the Stoics to the Cyrenaics, was ever afterward known as "the deserter." It was as difficult to be independent in philosophy as it is with us to be independent in politics. When a young man joined a school, he committed himself to all its opinions, not only as to the end of life, which was the main point of division, but as to all questions on all subjects. The Stoic did not differ merely in his ethics from the Epicurean; he differed also in his theology and his physics and his metaphysics. Aristotle, as Shakespeare knew, thought young men "unfit to hear moral philosophy". And yet it was a question--or rather the question--of moral philosophy, the answer to which decided the young man's opinions on all other points. The language which Cicero sometimes uses about the seriousness of the choice made in early life and how a young man gets entrammelled by a school before he is really able to judge, reminds us of what we hear said nowadays about the danger of a young man's taking orders before his opinions are formed. To this it was replied that a young man only exercised the right of private judgment in selecting the authority whom he should follow, and, having once done that, trusted to him for all the rest. With the analogue of this contention also we are familiar in modern times. Cicero allows that there would be something in it, if the selection of the true philosopher did not above all things require the philosophic mind. But in those days it was probably the case, as it is now, that, if a man did not form speculative opinions in youth, the pressure of affairs would not leave him leisure to do so later.

The life span of Zeno, the founder of Stoicism, was from B.C. 347 to 275. He did not begin teaching till 315, at the mature age of forty. Aristotle had passed away in 322, and with him closed the great constructive era of Greek thought. The Ionian philosophers had speculated on the physical constitution of the universe, the Pythagoreans on the mystical properties of numbers; Heraclitus had propounded his philosophy of fire, Democritus and Leucippus had struck out a rude form of the atomic theory, Socrates had raised questions relating to man, Plato had discussed them with all the freedom of the dialogue, while Aristotle had systematically worked them out. The later schools did not add much to the body of philosophy. What they did was to emphasize different sides of the doctrine of their predecessors and to drive views to their logical consequences. The great lesson of Greek philosophy is that it is worth while to do right irrespective of reward and punishment and regardless of the shortness of life. This lesson the Stoics so enforced by the earnestness of their lives and the influence of their moral teaching that it has become associated more particularly with them. Cicero, though he always classed himself as an Academic, exclaims in one place that he is afraid the Stoics are the only philosophers, and whenever he is combating Epicureanism his language is that of a Stoic. Some of Vergil's most eloquent passages seem to be inspired by Stoic speculation. Even Horace, despite his banter about the sage, in his serious moods borrows the language of the Stoics. It was they who inspired the highest flights of declamatory eloquence in Persius and Juvenal. Their moral philosophy affected the world through Roman law, the great masters of which were brought up under its influence. So all pervasive indeed was this moral philosophy of the Stoics that it was read by the Jews of Alexandria into Moses under the veil of allegory and was declared to be the inner meaning of the Hebrew Scriptures. If the Stoics then did not add much to the body of Philosophy, they did a great work in popularising it and bringing it to bear upon life.

An intense practicality was a mark of the later Greek philosophy. This was common to Stoicism with its rival Epicureanism. Both regarded philosophy as 'the art of life,' though they differed in their conception of what that art should be. Widely as the two schools were opposed to one another, they had also other features in common. Both were children of an age in which the free city had given way to monarchies, and personal had taken the place of corporate life. The question of happiness is no longer, as with Aristotle, and still more with Plato, one for the state, but for the individual. In both schools the speculative interest was feeble from the first, and tended to become feebler as time went on. Both were new departures from pre-existent schools. Stoicism was bred out of Cynicism, as Epicureanism out of Cyrenaicism. Both were content to fall back for their physics upon the pre-Socratic schools, the one adopting the firm philosophy of Heraclitus, the other the atomic theory of Democritus. Both were in strong reaction against the abstractions of Plato and Aristotle, and would tolerate nothing but concrete reality. The Stoics were quite as materialistic in their own way as the Epicureans. With regard indeed to the nature of the highest god we may, with Senaca represent the difference between the two schools as a question of the senses against the intellect, but we shall see presently that the Stoics regarded the intellect itself as being a kind of body.

The Greeks were all agreed that there was an end or aim of life, and that it was to be called 'happiness,' but at that point their agreement ended. As to the nature of happiness there was the utmost variety of opinion. Democritus had made it consist in mental serenity, Anaxagoras in speculation, Socrates in wisdom, Aristotle in the practise of virtue with some amount of favour from fortune, Aristippus simply in pleasure. These were opinions of the philosophers. But, besides these, there were the opinions of ordinary men, as shown by their lives rather than by their language. Zeno's contribution to thought on the subject does not at first sight appear illuminating. He said that the end was 'to live consistently,' the implication doubtless being that no life but the passionless life of reason could ultimately be consistent with itself. Cleanthes, his immediate successor in the school, is credited with having added the words 'with nature,' thus completing the well-known Stoic formula that the end is 'to live consistently with nature.'

It was assumed by the Greeks that the ways of nature were 'the ways of pleasantness,' and that 'all her paths' were 'peace.' This may seem to us a startling assumption, but that is because we do not mean by 'nature' the same thing as they did. We connect the term with the origin of a thing, they connected it rather with the end; by the 'natural state' we mean a state of savagery, they meant the highest civilization; we mean by a thing's nature what it is or has been, they meant what it ought to become under the most favourable conditions; not the sour crab, but the mellow glory of the Hesperides worthy to be guarded by a sleepless dragon, was to the Greeks the natural apple. Hence we find Aristotle maintaining that the State is a natural product, because it is evolved out of social relations which exist by nature. Nature indeed was a highly ambiguous term to the Greeks no less than to ourselves, but in the sense with which we are now concerned, the nature of anything was defined by the Peripatetics as 'the end of its becoming.' Another definition of theirs puts the matter still more clearly. 'What each thing is when its growth has been completed, that we declare to be the nature of each thing'.

Following out this conception the Stoics identified a life in accordance with nature with a life in accordance with the highest perfection to which man could attain. Now, as man was essentially a rational animal, his work as man lay in living the rational life. And the perfection of reason was virtue. Hence the ways of nature were no other than the ways of virtue. And so it came about that the Stoic formula might be expressed in a number of different ways which yet all amounted to the same thing. The end was to live the virtuous life, or to live consistently, or to live in accordance with nature, or to live rationally.

PHILOSOPHY AMONG THE GREEKS AND ROMANS.

DIVISION OF PHILOSOPHY.

Philosophy was defined by the Stoics as 'the knowledge of things divine and human'. It was divided into three departments; logic, ethic, and physic. This division indeed was in existence before their time, but they have got the credit of it as of some other things which they did not originate. Neither was it confined to them, but was part of the common stock of thought. Even the Epicureans, who are said to have rejected logic can hardly be counted as dissentients from this threefold division. For what they did was to substitute for the Stoic logic a logic of their own, dealing with the notions derived from sense, much in the same way as Bacon substituted his Novum Organum for the Organon of Aristotle. Cleanthes we are told recognised six parts of philosophy, namely, dialectic, rhetoric, ethic, politic, physic, and theology, but these are obviously the result of subdivision of the primary ones. Of the three departments we may say that logic deals with the form and expression of knowledge, physic with the matter of knowledge, and ethic with the use of knowledge. The division may also be justified in this way. Philosophy must study either nature (including the divine nature) or man; and, if it studies man, it must regard him either from the side of the intellect or of the feelings, that is either as a thinking (logic) or as an acting (ethic) being.

As to the order in which the different departments should he studied, we have had preserved to us the actual words of Chrysippus in his fourth book on Lives. 'First of all then it seems to me that, as has been

DIVISION OF PHILOSOPHY.

rightly said by the ancients, there are three heads under which the speculations of the philosopher fall, logic, ethic, physic; next, that of these the logical should come first, the ethical second, and the physical third, and that of the physical the treatment of the gods should come last, whence also they have given the name of "completions" to the instruction delivered on this subject'. That this order however might yield to convenience is plain from another book on the use of reason, where he says that 'the student who takes up logic first need not entirely abstain from the other branches of philosophy, but should study them also as occasion offers.'

Plutarch twits Chrysippus with inconsistency, because in the face of this declaration as to the order of treatment, he nevertheless says that morals rest upon physics. But to this charge it may fairly be replied that the order of exposition need not coincide with the order of existence. Metaphysically speaking, morals may depend upon physics and the right conduct of man be deducible from the structure of the universe but for all that, it may be advisable to study physics later. Physics meant the nature of God and the Universe. Our nature may be deducible from that but it is better known to ourselves to start with, so that it may be well to begin from the end of the stick that we have in our hands. But that Chrysippus did teach the logical dependence of morals on physics is plain from his own words. In his third book on the Gods he says 'for it is not possible to find any other origin of justice or mode of its generation save that from Zeus and the nature of the universe for anything we have to say about good and evil must needs derive its origin therefrom', and again in his Physical Theses, 'for there is no other or more appropriate way of approaching the subject of good and evil on the virtues or happiness than from the nature of all things and the administration of the universe--for it is to these we must attach the treatment of good and evil inasmuch as there is no better origin to which we can refer them and inasmuch as physical speculation is taken in solely with a view to the distinction between good and evil.'

The last words are worth noting as showing that even with Chrysippus who has been called the intellectual founder of Stoicism the whole stress of the philosophy of the Porch fell upon its moral teaching. It was a favourite metaphor with the school to compare philosophy to a fertile vineyard or orchard. Ethic was the good fruit, physic the tall plants, and logic the strong wall. The wall existed only to guard the trees, and the trees only to produce the fruit. Or again philosophy was likened to an egg of which ethic was the yolk containing the chick, physic the white which formed its nourishment while logic was the hard outside shell. Posidonius, a later member of the school, objected to the metaphor from the vineyard on the ground that the fruit and the trees and the wall were all separable whereas the parts of philosophy were inseparable. He preferred therefore to liken it to a living organism, logic being the bones and sinews, physic the flesh and blood, but ethic the soul

DIVISION OF PHILOSOPHY.

LOGIC

The Stoics had a tremendous reputation for logic. In this department they were the successors or rather the supersessors of Aristotle. For after the death of Theophrastus the library of the Lyceum is said to have been buried underground at Scepsis until about a century before Christ, So that the Organon may actually have been lost to the world during that period. At all events under Strato the successor of Theophrastus who specialized in natural science the school had lost its comprehensiveness. Cicero even finds it consonant with dramatic propriety to make Cato charge the later Peripatetics with ignorance of logic! On the other hand Chrysippus became so famous for his logic as to create a general impression that if there were a logic among the gods it would be no other than the Chrysippean.

But if the Stoics were strong in logic they were weak in rhetoric. This strength and weakness were characteristic of the school at all periods. Cato is the only Roman Stoic to whom Cicero accords the praise of real eloquence. In the dying accents of the school as we hear them in Marcus Aurelius the imperial sage counts it a thing to be thankful for that he had learnt to abstain from rhetoric, poetic, and elegance of diction. The reader however cannot help wishing that he had taken some means to diminish the crabbedness of his style. If a lesson were wanted in the importance of sacrificing to the Graces it might be found in the fact that the early Stoic writers despite their logical subtlety have all perished and that their remains have to be sought for so largely in the pages of Cicero. In speaking of logic as one of the three departments of philosophy we must bear in mind that the term was one of much wider meaning than it is with us. It included rhetoric, poetic, and grammar as well as dialectic or logic proper, to say nothing of disquisitions on the senses and the intellect which we should now refer to psychology.

Logic as a whole being divided into rhetoric and dialectic: rhetoric was defined to be the knowledge of how to speak well in expository discourses and dialectic as the knowledge of how to argue rightly in matters of question and answer. Both rhetoric and dialectic were spoken of by the Stoics as virtues for they divided virtue in its most generic sense in the same way as they divided philosophy into physical, ethical, and logical. Rhetoric and dialectic were thus the two species of logical virtue. Zeno expressed their difference by comparing rhetoric to the palm and dialectic to the fist.

Instead of throwing in poetic and grammar with rhetoric, the Stoics subdivided dialectic into the part which dealt with the meaning and the part which dealt with the sound, or as Chrysippus phrased it, concerning significants and significates. Under the former came the treatment of the alphabet, of the parts of speech, of solecism, of barbarism, of poems, of amphibolies, of metre and music--a list which seems at first sight a little mixed, but in which we can recognise the general features of grammar, with its departments of phonology, accidence, and prosody. The treatment of solecism and barbarism in grammar corresponded to that of fallacies in logic. With regard to the alphabet it is worth noting that the Stoics recognised seven vowels and six mutes. This is more correct than our way of talking of nine mutes, since the aspirate consonants are plainly not mute. There were, according to the Stoics, five parts of speech--name, appellative, verb, conjunction, article. 'Name' meant a proper name, and 'appellative' a common term.

There were reckoned to be five virtues of speech--Hellenism, clearness, conciseness, propriety, distinction. By 'Hellenism' was meant speaking good Greek. 'Distinction' was defined to be 'a diction which avoided homeliness.' Over against these there were two comprehensive vices, barbarism and solecism, the one being an offence against accidence, the other against syntax.

The famous comparison of the infant mind to a blank sheet of paper, which we connect so closely with the name of Locke, really comes from the Stoics. The earliest characters inscribed upon it were the impressions of sense, which the Greeks called "phantasies." A phantasy was defined by Zeno as "an impression in the soul." Cleanthes was content to take this definition in its literal sense, and believe that the soul was impressed by external objects as wax by a signet ring. Chrysippus, however, found a difficulty here, and preferred to interpret the Master's saying to mean an alteration or change in the soul. He figured to himself the soul as receiving a modification from every external object which acts upon it just as the air receives countless strokes when many people are speaking at once. Further, he declared that in receiving an impression the soul was purely passive and that the phantasy revealed not only its own existence, but that also of its cause, just as light displays itself and the things that are in it. Thus, when through sight we receive an impression of white, an affection takes place in the soul, in virtue whereof we are able to say that there exists a white object affecting us. The power to name the object resides in the understanding. First must come the phantasy, and the understanding, having the power of utterance, expresses in speech the affection it receives from the object. The cause of the phantasy was called the "phantast," _e. g._ the white or cold object. If there is no external cause, then the supposed object of the impression was a "phantasm," such as a figure in a dream, or the Furies whom Orestes sees in his frenzy.

How then was the impression which had reality behind it to be distinguished from that which had not? "By the feel" is all that the Stoics really had to say in answer to this question. Just as Hume made the difference between sense-impressions and ideas to lie in the greater vividness of the former, so did they; only Hume saw no necessity to go beyond the impression, whereas the Stoics did. Certain impressions, they maintained, carried with them an irresistible conviction of their own reality, and this, not merely in the sense that they existed; but also that they were referable to an external cause. These were called "gripping phantasies." Such a phantasy did not need proof of its own existence, or of that of its object. It possessed self-evidence. Its occurrence was attended with yielding and assent on the part of the soul. For it is as natural for the soul to assent to the self-evident as it is for it to pursue its proper good. The assent to a griping phantasy was called "comprehension," as indicating the firm hold that the soul thus took of reality. A gripping phantasy was defined as one which was stamped and impressed from an existing object, in virtue of that object itself, in such a way as it could not be from a non-existent object. The clause "in virtue of that object itself" was put into the definition to provide against such a case as that of the mad Orestes, who takes his sister to be a Fury. There the impression was derived from an existing object, but not from that object as such, but as coloured by the imagination of the percipient.

The criterion of truth then was no other than the gripping phantasy. Such at least was the doctrine of the earlier Stoics, but the later added a saving clause, "when there is no impediment." For they were pressed by their opponents with such imaginary cases as that of Admetus, seeing his wife before him in very deed, and yet not believing it to be her. But here there was an impediment. Admetus did not believe that the dead could rise. Again Menelaus did not believe in the real Helen when he found her on the island of Pharos. But here again there was an impediment. For Menelaus could not have been expected to know that he had been for ten years fighting for a phantom. When, however, there was no such impediment, then they said the gripping phantasy did indeed deserve its name, for it almost took men by the hair of the head and dragged them to assent.

So far we have used "phantasy" only of real or imaginary impressions of sense. But the term was not thus restricted by the Stoics, who divided phantasies into sensible and not sensible. The latter came through the understanding and were of bodiless things which could only be grasped by reason. The ideas of Plato they declared existed only in our minds. Horse, man, and animal had no substantial existence but were phantasms of the soul. The Stoics were thus what we should call Conceptualists.

Comprehension too was used in a wider sense than that in which we have so far employed it. There was comprehension by the senses as of white and black, of rough and smooth, but there was also comprehension by the reason of demonstrative conclusions such as that the gods exist and that they exercise providence. Here we are reminded of Locke's declaration: "'Tis as certain there's a God as that the opposite angles made by the intersection of two straight lines are equal." The Stoics indeed had great affinities with that thinker or rather he with them. The Stoic account of the manner in which the mind arrives at its ideas might almost be taken from the first book of Locke's _Essay_. As many as nine ways are enumerated of which the first corresponds to simple ideas--

(1) by presentation, as objects of sense

(2) by likeness, as the idea of Socrates from his picture

(3) by analogy, that is, by increase or decrease, as ideas of giants and pigmies from men, or as the notion of the centre of the earth, which is reached by the consideration of smaller spheres.

(4) by transposition, as the idea of men with eyes in their breasts.

(5) by composition, as the idea of a Centaur.

(6) by opposition, as the idea of death from that of life.

(7) by a kind of transition, as the meaning of words and the idea of place.

(8) by nature, as the notion of the just and the good

(9) by privation, as handless

The Stoics resembled Locke again in endeavoring to give such a definition of knowledge as should cover at once the reports of the senses and the relation between ideas. Knowledge was defined by them as a sure comprehension or a habit in the acceptance of phantasies which was not liable to be changed by reason. On a first hearing these definitions might seem limited to sense knowledge but if we bethink ourselves of the wider meanings of comprehension and of phantasy, we see that the definitions apply as they were meant to apply to the mind's grasp upon the force of a demonstration no less than upon the existence of a physical object.

Zeno, with that touch of oriental symbolism which characterized him, used to illustrate to his disciples the steps to knowledge by means of gestures. Displaying his right hand with the fingers outstretched he would say, "That is a phantasy," then contracting the fingers a little, "That is assent," then having closed the fist, "That is comprehension," then clasping the fist closely with the left hand, he would add, "That is knowledge."

A notion which corresponds to our word concept was defined as a phantasm of the understanding of a rational animal. For a notion was but a phantasm as it presented itself to a rational mind. In the same way so many shillings and sovereigns are in themselves but shillings and sovereigns, but when used as passage money they become fare. Notions were arrived at partly by nature, partly by teaching and study. The former kind of notions were called preconceptions; the latter went merely by the generic name.

Out of the general ideas which nature imparts to us, reason was perfected about the age of fourteen, at the time when the voice--its outward and visible sign--attains its full development, and when the human animal is complete in other respects as being able to reproduce its kind. Thus reason which united us to the gods was not, according to the Stoics, a pre-existent principal, but a gradual development out of sense. It might truly be said that with them the senses were the intellect.

Being was confined by the Stoics to body, a bold assertion of which we shall meet the consequences later. At present it is sufficient to notice what havoc it makes among the categories. Of Aristotle's ten categories it leaves only the first, Substance, and that only in its narrowest sense of Primary Substance. But a substance or body might be regarded in four ways-- (1) simply as a body (2) as a body of a particular kind (3) as a body in a particular state (4) as a body in a particular relation.

Hence result the four Stoic categories of-- substrates suchlike so disposed so related

But the bodiless would not be thus conjured out of existence. For what was to be made of such things as the meaning of words, time, place, and the infinite void? Even the Stoics did not assign body to these, and yet they had to be recognized and spoken of. The difficulty was got over by the invention of the higher category of somewhat, which should include both body and the bodiless. Time was a somewhat, and so was space, though neither of them possessed being.

In the Stoic treatment of the proposition, grammar was very much mixed up with logic. They had a wide name which applied to any part of diction, whether a word or words, a sentence, or even a syllogism. This we shall render by "dict." A dict, then, was defined as "that which subsists in correspondence with a rational phantasy." A dict was one of the things which the Stoics admitted to be devoid of body. There were three things involved when anything was said--the sound, the sense, and the external object. Of these the first and the last were bodies, but the intermediate one was not a body. This we may illustrate after Seneca, as follows: "You see Cato walking. What your eyes see and your mind attends to is a body in motion. Then you say, 'Cato is walking'." The mere sound indeed of these words is air in motion and therefore a body but the meaning of them is not a body but an enouncement about a body, which is quite a different thing.

On examining such details as are left us of the Stoic logic, the first thing which strikes one is its extreme complexity as compared with the Aristotelian. It was a scholastic age, and the Stoics refined and distinguished to their hearts' content. As regards immediate inference, a subject which has been run into subtleties among ourselves, Chrysippus estimated that the changes which could be rung on ten propositions exceeded a million, but for this assertion he was taken to task by Hipparchus the mathematician, who proved that the affirmative proposition yielded exactly 103,049 forms and the negative 310,962. With us the affirmative proposition is more prolific in consequences than the negative. But then, the Stoics were not content with so simple a thing as mere negation, but had negative arnetic and privative, to say nothing of supernegative propositions. Another noticeable feature is the total absence of the three figures of Aristotle and the only moods spoken of are the moods of the complex syllogism, such as the _modus penens_ in a conjunctive. Their type of reasoning was-- If A, then B But A B

The important part played by conjunctive propositions in their logic led the Stoics to formulate the following rule with regard to the material quality of such propositions: Truth can only be followed by truth, but falsehood may be followed by falsehood or truth.

Thus if it be truly stated that it is day, any consequence of that statement, _e.g._ that it is light, must be true also. But a false statement may lead either way. For instance, if it be falsely stated that it is night then the consequence that it is dark is false also. But if we say, "The earth flies," which was regarded as not only false but impossible [Footnote: Here we may recall the warning of Arago to call nothing impossible outside the range of pure mathematics] this involves the true consequence that the earth is. Though the simple syllogism is not alluded to in the sketch which Diogenes Laertius gives of the Stoic logic, it is of frequent occurrence in the accounts left us of their arguments. Take for instance the syllogism wherewith Zeno advocated the cause of temperance-- One does not commit a secret to a man who is drunk. One does commit a secret to a good man. A good man will not get drunk.

The chain argument which we wrongly call the Sorites was also a favorite resource with the Stoics. If a single syllogism did not suffice to argue men into virtue surely a condensed series must be effectual. And so they demonstrated the sufficiency of wisdom for happiness as follows---- The wise man is temperate The temperate is constant The constant is unperturbed The unperturbed is free from sorrow Whoso is free from sorrow is happy The wise man is happy

The delight which the early Stoics took in this pure play of the intellect led them to pounce with avidity upon the abundant stock of fallacies current among the Greeks of their time. These seem--most of them--to have been invented by the Megarians and especially by Eubulides of Miletus a disciple of Eucleides but they became associated with the Stoics both by friends and foes who either praise their subtlety or deride their solemnity in dealing with them. Chrysippus himself was not above propounding such sophisms as the following--

   Whoever divulges the mysteries to the uninitiated commits impiety The hierophant divulged the mysteries to the uninitiated The hierophant commits impiety

   Anything that you say passes through your mouth You say a wagon A wagon passes through your mouth

He is said to have written eleven books on the No-one fallacy. But what seems to have exercised most of his ingenuity was the famous Liar, the invention of which is ascribed to Eubulides. This fallacy in its simplest form is as follows. If you say truly that you are telling a lie, are you lying or telling the truth? Chrysippus set this down as inexplicable. Nevertheless he was far from declining to discuss it. For we find in the list of his works a treatise in five books on the Inexplicables an Introduction to the Liar and Liars for Introduction, six books on the Liar itself, a work directed against those who thought that such propositions were both false and true, another against those who professed to solve the Liar by a process of division, three books on the solution of the Liar, and finally a polemic against those who asserted that the Liar had its premises false. It was well for poor Philetas of Cos that he ended his days before Chrysippus was born, though as it was he grew thin and died of the Liar, and his epitaph served as a solemn reminder to poets not to meddle with logic--

Philetas of Cos am I   'Twas the Liar who made me die   And the bad nights caused thereby.

Perhaps we owe him an apology for the translation.

ETHIC

We have already had to touch upon the psychology of the Stoics in connection with the first principles of logic. It is no less necessary to do so now in dealing with the foundation of ethic.

The Stoics we are told reckoned that there were eight parts of the soul. These were the five senses, the organ of sound, the intellect and the reproductive principle. The passions, it will be observed, are conspicuous by their absence. For the Stoic theory was that the passions were simply the intellect in a diseased state owing to the perversions of falsehood. This is why the Stoics would not parley with passion, conceiving that if once it were let into the citadel of the soul it would supplant the rightful ruler. Passion and reason were not two things which could be kept separate in which case it might be hoped that reason would control passion, but were two states of the same thing--a worse and a better.

The unperturbed intellect was the legitimate monarch in the kingdom of man. Hence the Stoics commonly spoke of it as the leading principle. This was the part of the soul which received phantasies and it was also that in which impulses were generated with which we have now more particularly to do.

Impulse or appetition was the principle in the soul which impelled to action. In an unperverted state it was directed only to things in accordance with nature. The negative form of this principle or the avoidance of things as being contrary to nature, we shall call repulsion.

Notwithstanding the sublime heights to which Stoic morality rose. It was professedly based on self-love, wherein the Stoics were at one with the other schools of thought in the ancient world.

The earliest impulse that appeared in a newly born animal was to protect itself and its own constitution which were conciliated to it by nature. What tended to its survival, it sought; what tended to its destruction, it shunned. Thus self-preservation was the first law of life.

While man was still in the merely animal stage, and before reason was developed in him, the things that were in accordance with his nature were such as health, strength, good bodily condition, soundness of all the senses, beauty, swiftness--in short all the qualities that went to make up richness of physical life and that contributed to the vital harmony. These were called the first things in accordance with nature. Their opposites were all contrary to nature, such as sickness, weakness, mutilation. Under the first things in accordance with nature came also congenial advantages of soul such as quickness of intelligence, natural ability, industry, application, memory, and the like. It was a question whether pleasure was to be included among the number. Some members of the school evidently though that it might be, but the orthodox opinion was that pleasure was a sort of aftergrowth and that the direct pursuit of it was deleterious to the organism. The after growths of virtue were joy, cheerfulness, and the like. These were the gambolings of the spirit like the frolicsomeness of an animal in the full flush of its vitality or like the blooming of a plant. For one and the same power manifested itself in all ranks of nature, only at each stage on a higher level. To the vegetative powers of the plant the animal added sense and Impulse. It was in accordance therefore with the nature of an animal to obey the Impulses of sense, but to sense and Impulse man superadded reason so that when he became conscious of himself as a rational being, it was in accordance with his nature to let all his Impulses be shaped by this new and master hand. Virtue was therefore pre-eminently in accordance with nature. What then we must now ask is the relation of reason to impulse as conceived by the Stoics? Is reason simply the guiding, and impulse the motive power? Seneca protests against this view, when impulse is identified with passion. One of his grounds for doing so is that reason would be put on a level with passion, if the two were equally necessary for action. But the question is begged by the use of the word 'passion,' which was defined by the Stoics as 'an excessive impulse.' Is it possible then, even on Stoic principles, for reason to work without something different from itself to help it? Or must we say that reason is itself a principle of action? Here Plutarch comes to our aid, who tells us on the authority of Chrysippus in his work on Law that impulse is 'the reason of man commanding him to act,' and similarly that repulsion is 'prohibitive reason.' This renders the Stoic position unmistakable, and we must accomodate our minds to it in spite of its difficulties. Just as we have seen already that reason is not something radically different from sense, so now it appears that reason is not different from impulse, but itself the perfected form of impulse. Whenever impulse is not identical with reason--at least in a rational being--it is not truly impulse, but passion.

The Stoics, it will be observed, were Evolutionists in their psychology. But, like many Evolutionists at the present day, they did not believe in the origin of mind out of matter. In all living things there existed already what they called 'seminal reasons,' which accounted for the intelligence displayed by plants as well as by animals. As there were four cardinal virtues, so there were four primary passions. These were delight, grief, desire and fear. All of them were excited by the presence or the prospect of fancied good or ill. What prompted desire by its prospect caused delight by its presence, and what prompted fear by its prospect caused grief by its presence. Thus two of the primary passions had to do with good and two with evil. All were furies which infested the life of fools, rendering it bitter and grievous to them; and it was the business of philosophy to fight against them. Nor was this strife a hopeless one, since the passions were not grounded in nature, but were due to false opinion. They originated in voluntary judgements, and owed their birth to a lack of mental sobriety. If men wished to live the span of life that was allotted to them in quietness and peace, they must by all means keep clear of the passions.

The four primary passions having been formulated, it became necessary to justify the division by arranging the specific forms of feeling under these four heads. In this task the Stoics displayed a subtlety which is of more interest to the lexicographer than to the student of philosophy. They laid great stress on the derivation of words as affording a clue to their meaning; and, as their etymology was bound by no principles, their ingenuity was free to indulge in the wildest freaks of fancy.

Though all passion stood self-condemned, there were nevertheless certain 'eupathies,' or happy affections, which would be experienced by the ideally good and wise man. These were not perturbations of the soul, but rather 'constancies'; they were not opposed to reason, but were rather part of reason. Though the sage would never be transported with delight, he would still feel an abiding 'joy' in the presence of the true and only good; he would never indeed be agitated by desire, but still he would be animated by 'wish,' for that was directed only to the good; and though he would never feel fear still he would be actuated in danger by a proper caution.

There was therefore something rational corresponding to three out of four primary passions--against delight was to be set joy; against grief there was nothing to be set, for that arose from the presence of ill which would rather never attach to the sage. Grief was the irrational conviction that one ought to afflict oneself where there was no occasion for it. The ideal of the Stoics was the unclouded serenity of Socrates of whom Xanthippe declared that he had always the same face whether on leaving the house In the morning or on returning to it at night.

As the motley crowd of passions followed the banners of their four leaders so specific forms of feeling sanctioned by reason were severally assigned to the three eupathies.

Things were divided by Zeno into good, bad, and indifferent. To good belonged virtue and what partook of virtue; to bad, vice and what partook of vice. All other things were indifferent.

To the third class then belonged such things as life and death, health and sickness, pleasure and pain, beauty and ugliness, strength and weakness, honour and dishonour, wealth and poverty, victory and defeat, nobility and baseness of birth.

Good was defined as that which benefits. To confer benefit was no less essential to good than to impart warmth was to heat. If one asked in what 'to benefit' lay one received the reply that it lay in producing an act or state in accordance with virtue, and similarly it was laid down that 'to hurt' lay in producing an act or state in accordance with vice.

The indifference of things other than virtue and vice was apparent from the definition of good which made it essentially beneficial. Such things as health and wealth might be beneficial or not according to circumstances; they were therefore no more good than bad. Again, nothing could be really good of which the good or ill depended on the use made of it, but this was the case with things like health and wealth.

The true and only good then was identical with what the Greeks called 'the beautiful' and what we call 'the right'. To say that a thing was right was to say that it was good, and conversely to say that it was good was to say that it was right; this absolute identity between the good and the right and, on the other hand, between the bad and wrong, was the head and front of the Stoic ethics. The right contained in itself all that was necessary for the happy life, the wrong was the only evil, and made men miserable whether they knew it or not.

As virtue was itself the end, it was of course choiceworthy in and for itself, apart from hope or fear with regard to its consequences. Moreover, as being the highest good, it could admit of no increase from the addition of things indifferent. It did not even admit of increase from the prolongation of its own existence, for the question was not one of quantity, but of quality. Virtue for an eternity was no more virtue, and therefore no more good, than virtue for a moment. Even so one circle was no more round than another, whatever you might choose to make its diameter, nor would it detract from the perfection of a circle if it were to be obliterated immediately in the same dust in which it had been drawn.

To say that the good of men lay in virtue was another way of saying that it lay in reason, since virtue was the perfection of reason.

As reason was the only thing whereby Nature had distinguished man from other creatures, to live the rational life was to follow Nature.

Nature was at once the law of God and the law for man. For by the nature of anything was meant, not that which we actually find it to be, but that which in the eternal fitness of things it was obviously intended to become.

To be happy then was to be virtuous, to be virtuous was to be rational, to be rational was to follow Nature, and to follow Nature was to obey God. Virtue imparted to life that even flow in which Zeno declared happiness to consist. This was attained when one's own genius was in harmony with the will that disposed of all things.

Virtue having been purified from all the dross of the emotions, came out as something purely intellectual, so that the Stoics agreed with the Socratic conception that virtue is knowledge. They also took on from Plato the four cardinal virtues of Wisdom, Temperance, Courage, and Justice, and defined them as so many branches of knowledge. Against these were set four cardinal vices of Folly, Intemperance, Cowardice, and Injustice. Under both the virtues and vices there was an elaborate classification of specific qualities. But notwithstanding the care with which the Stoics divided and subdivided the virtues, virtue, according to their doctrine, was all the time one and indivisible. For virtue was simply reason and reason, if it were there, must control every department of conduct alike. 'He who has one virtue has all,' was a paradox with which the Greek thought was already familiar. But Chrysippus went beyond this, declaring that he who displayed one virtue did thereby display all. Neither was the man perfect who did not possess all the virtues, nor was the act perfect which did not involve them all. Where the virtues differed from one another was merely in the order in which they put things. Each was primarily itself, secondarily all the rest. Wisdom had to determine what it was right to do, but this involved the other virtues. Temperance had to impart stability to the impulses, but how could the term 'temperate' be applied to a man who deserted his post through cowardice, or who failed to return a deposit through avarice, which is a form of injustice, or yet to one who misconducted affairs through rashness, which falls under folly? Courage had to face dangers and difficulties, but it was not courage unless its cause were just. Indeed one of the ways in which courage was defined was a virtue fighting on behalf of justice. Similarly justice put first the assigning to each man his due, but in the act of doing so had to bring in the other virtues. In short, it was the business of the man of virtue to know and to do what ought to be done, for what ought to be done implied wisdom in choice, courage in endurance, justice in assignment and temperance in abiding by ones conviction. One virtue never acted by itself, but always on the advice of a committee. The obverse to this paradox--He who has one vice has all vices--was a conclusion which the Stoics did not shrink from drawing. One might lose part of one's Corinthian ware and still retain the rest, but to lose one virtue--if virtue could be lost--would be to lose all along with it.

We have now encountered the first paradox of Stoicism, and can discern its origin in the identification of virtue with pure reason. In getting forth the novelties in Zeno's teaching, Cicero mentions that, while his predecessors had recognized virtues due to nature and habit, he made all dependent upon reason. A natural consequence of this was the reassertion of the position which Plato held or wished to hold, namely, that virtue can be taught. But the part played by nature in virtue cannot be ignored. It was not in the power of Zeno to alter facts. All he could do was to legislate as to names. And this he did vigorously. Nothing was to be called virtue which was not of the nature of reason and knowledge, but still it had to be admitted that nature supplied the starting points for the four cardinal virtues--for the discovery of one's impulses, for right endurances and harmonious distributions.

From things good and bad we now turn to things indifferent. Hitherto the Stoic doctrine has been stern and uncompromising. We have now to look at it under a different aspect, and to see how it tried to conciliate common sense.

By things indifferent were meant such as did not necessarily contribute to virtue, for instance health, wealth, strength, and honor. It is possible to have all these and not be virtuous, it is possible also to be virtuous without them. But we have now to learn that though these things are neither good nor evil, and are therefore not matter for choice or avoidance, they are far from being indifferent in the sense of arousing neither impulse nor repulsion. There are things indeed that are indifferent in the latter sense, such as whether you put out your finger this way or that, whether you stoop to pick up a straw or not, whether the number of hairs on your head be odd or even. But things of this sort are exceptional. The bulk of things other than virtue and vice do arouse in us either impulse or repulsion. Let it be understood then that there are two senses of the word indifferent-- (1) neither good nor bad (2) neither awaking impulse nor repulsion

Among things indifferent in the former sense, some were in accordance with nature, some were contrary to nature and some were neither one nor the other. Health, strengths and soundness of the senses were in accordance with nature; sickness weakness and mutilation were contrary to nature, but such things as the fallibility of the soul and the vulnerability of the body were neither in accordance with nature nor yet contrary to nature, but just nature.

All things that were in accordance with nature had 'value' and all things that were contrary to nature had what we must call 'disvalue'. In the highest sense indeed of the term 'value'--namely that of absolute value or worth--things indifferent did not possess any value at all. But still there might be assigned to them what Antipater expressed by the term 'a selective value' or what he expressed by its barbarous privative, 'a disselective disvalue'. If a thing possessed a selective value you took that thing rather than its contrary, supposing that circumstances allowed, for instance, health rather than sickness, wealth rather than poverty, life rather than death. Hence such things were called takeable and their contraries untakeable. Things that possessed a high degree of value were called preferred, those that possessed a high degree of disvalue were called rejected. Such as possessed no considerable degree of either were neither preferred nor rejected. Zeno, with whom these names originated, justified their use about things really indifferent on the ground that at court "preferment" could not be bestowed upon the king himself, but only on his ministers.

Things preferred and rejected might belong to mind, body or estate. Among things preferred in the case of the mind were natural ability, art, moral progress, and the like, while their contraries were rejected. In the case of the body, life, health, strength, good condition, completeness, and beauty were preferred, while death, sickness, weakness, ill condition, mutilation and ugliness were rejected. Among things external to soul and body, wealth, reputation, and nobility were preferred, while poverty, ill repute, and baseness of birth were rejected.

In this way all mundane and marketable goods, after having been solemnly refused admittance by the Stoics at the front door, were smuggled in at a kind of tradesman's entrance under the name of things indifferent. We must now see how they had, as it were, two moral codes, one for the sage and the other for the world in general.

The sage alone could act rightly, but other people might perform "the proprieties." Any one might honor his parents, but the sage alone did it as the outcome of wisdom, because he alone possessed the art of life, the peculiar work of which was to do everything that was done as the result of the best disposition. All the acts of the sage were "perfect proprieties," which were called "rightnesses." All acts of all other men were sins or "wrongnesses." At their best they could only be "intermediate proprieties." The term "propriety," then, is a generic one. But, as often happens, the generic term got determined in use to a specific meaning, so that intermediate acts are commonly spoken of as "proprieties" in opposition to "rightnesses." Instances of "rightnesses" are displaying wisdom and dealing justly, instances of proprieties or intermediate acts are marrying, going on an embassy, and dialectic.

The word "duty" is often employed to translate the Greek term which we are rendering by "propriety." Any translation is no more than a choice of evils, since we have no real equivalent for the term. It was applicable not merely to human conduct, but also to the acting of the lower animals, and even to the growth of plants. Now, apart from a craze of generalization we should hardly think of the "stern daughter of the voice of God" in connection with an amoeba corresponding successfully to stimulus, yet the creature in its inchoate way is exhibiting a dim analogy to duty. The term in question was first used by Zeno, and was explained by him, in accordance with its etymology, to mean what it came to one to do, so that as far as this goes, 'becomingness' would be the most appropriate translation.

The sphere of propriety was confined to things indifferent, so that there were proprieties which were common to the sage and the fool. It had to do with taking the things which were in accordance with nature and rejecting those that were not. Even the propriety of living or dying was determined, not by reference to virtue or vice, but to the preponderance or deficiency of things in accordance with nature. It might thus be a propriety for the sage in spite of his happiness, to depart from life of his own accord, and for the fool notwithstanding his misery, to remain in it. Life, being in itself indifferent, the whole question was one of opportunism. Wisdom might prompt the leaving herself should occasion seem to call for it.

We pass on now another instance of accommodation. According to the high Stoic doctrine, there was no mean between virtue and vice. All men indeed received from nature the starting-points for virtue, but until perfection had been attained they rested under the condemnation of vice. It was, to employ an illustration of the poet-philosopher Cleanthes, as though Nature had begun an iambic line and left men to finish it. Until that was done they were to wear the fool's cap. The Peripatetics, on the other hand, recognized an intermediate state between virtue and vice, to which they gave the name of progress and proficience. Yet so entirely had the Stoics, for practical purposes, to accept this lower level, that the word "proficience" has come to be spoken of as though it were of Stoic origin.

Seneca is fond of contrasting the sage with the proficient. The sage is like a man in the enjoyment of perfect health. But the proficient is like a man recovering from a severe illness, with whom an abatement of the paroxysm is equivalent to health, and who is always in danger of a relapse. It is the business of philosophy to provide for the needs of these weaker brethren. The proficient is still called a fool, but it is pointed out that he is a very different kind of fool from the rest. Further, proficients are arranged into three classes, in a way that reminds one of the technicalities of Calvinistic theology. First of all, there are those who are near wisdom, but, however near they may be to the door of Heaven, they are still on the wrong side of it. According to some doctors, these were already safe from backsliding, differing from the sage only in not having yet realized that they had attained to knowledge; other authorities, however, refused to admit this, and regarded the first class as being exempt only from settled diseases of the soul, but not from passing attacks of passion. Thus did the Stoics differ among themselves as to the doctrine of "final assurance". The second class consisted of those who had laid aside the worst diseases and passions of the soul, but might at any moment relapse into them. The third class was of those who had escaped one mental malady but not another; who had conquered lust, let us say, but not ambition; who disregarded death, but dreaded pain, This third class, adds Seneca, is by no means to be despised.

From these concessions to the weakness of humanity we now pass to the Stoic paradoxes, where we shall see their doctrine in its full rigor. It is perhaps these very paradoxes which account for the puzzled fascination with which Stoicism affected the mind of antiquity, just as obscurity in a poet may prove a surer passport to fame than more strictly poetical merits.

The root of Stoicism being a paradox, it is not surprising that the offshoots should be so too. To say that "Virtue is the highest good" is a proposition to which every one who aspires to the spiritual life must yield assent with his lips, even if he has not yet learned to believe it in his heart. But alter it into "Virtue is the only good" and by that slight change it becomes at once the teeming mother of paradoxes. By a paradox is meant that which runs counter to general opinion. Now it is quite certain that men have regarded, do regard, and, we may safely add will regard things as good which are not virtue. But if we grant this initial paradox, a great many others will follow along with it--as for instance that "Virtue is sufficient of itself for happiness". The fifth book of Cicero's _Tusculan Disputations_ is an eloquent defense of this thesis, in which the orator combats the suggestion that a good man is not happy when he is being broken on the wheel.

Another glaring paradox of the Stoics is that "All faults are equal". They took their stand upon a mathematical conception of rectitude. An angle must be either a right angle or not, a line must be either straight or crooked, so an act must be either right or wrong. There is no mean between the two and there are no degrees of either. To sin is to cross the line. When once that has been done it makes no difference to the offense how far you go. Trespassing at all is forbidden. This doctrine was defended by the Stoics on account of its bracing moral effect as showing the heinousness of sin. Horace gives the judgment of the world in saying that common sense and morality, to say nothing of utility, revolt against it.

Here are some other specimens of the Stoic paradoxes. "Every fool is mad". "Only the sage is free and every fool is a slave". "The sage alone is wealthy". "Good men are always happy and bad men always miserable". "All goods are equal". "No one is wiser or happier than another". But may not one man we ask be more nearly wise or more nearly happy than another? "That may be", the Stoics would reply, "but the man who is only one stade from Canopus is as much not in Canopus as the man who is a hundred stades off; and the eight day old puppy is still as blind as on the day of its birth; nor can a man who is near the surface of the sea breathe any more than if he were full five hundred fathom down".

It is only fair to the Stoics to add that paradoxes were quite the order of the day in Greece, though they greatly outdid other schools in producing them. Socrates himself was the father of paradox. Epicurus maintained as staunchly as any Stoic that "No wise man is unhappy", and, if he be not belied, went the length of declaring that the wise man, if put into the bull of Phalaris would exclaim: "How delightful! How little I mind this!"

It is out of keeping with common sense to draw a hard and fast distinction between good and bad. Yet this was what the Stoics did. They insisted on effecting here and now that separation between the sheep and the goats, which Christ postponed to the Day of Judgment. Unfortunately, when it came to practice, all were found to be goats, so that the division was a merely formal one.

The good man of the Stoics was variously known as 'the sage', or, 'the serious man', the latter name being inherited from the Peripatetics. We

ETHIC

used to hear it said among ourselves that a person had become serious, when he or she had taken to religion. Another appellation which the Stoics had for the sage was 'the urbane man', while the fool in contradistinction was called 'a boor'. Boorishness was defined as an inexperience of the customs and laws of the state. By the state was meant, not Athens or Sparta, as would have been the case in a former age, but the society of all rational beings into which the Stoics spiritualised the state. The sage alone had the freedom of this city and the fool was therefore not only a boor, but an alien or an exile. In this city, Justice was natural and not conventional, for the law by which it was governed was the law of right reason. The law then was spiritualised by the Stoics, just as the state was. It no longer meant the enactments of this or that community, but the mandates of the eternal reason which ruled the world and which would prevail in the ideal state. Law was defined as right reason commanding what was to be done and forbidding what was not to be done. As such, it in no way differed from the impulse of the sage himself.

As a member of a state and by nature subject to law, man was essentially a social being. Between all the wise there existed "unanimity," which was "a knowledge of the common good," because their views of life were harmonious. Fools, on the other hand, whose views of life were discordant, were enemies to one another and bent on mutual injury.

As a member of society the sage would play his part in public life. Theoretically this was always true, and practically he would do so, wherever the actual constitution made any tolerable approach to the ideal type. But, if the circumstances were such as to make it certain that his embarking on politics would be of no service to his country, and only a source of danger to himself, then he would refrain. The kind of constitution of which the Stoics most approved was a mixed government containing democratic, aristocratic, and monarchical elements. Where circumstances allowed the sage would act as legislator, and would educate mankind, one way of doing which was by writing books which would prove of profit to the reader.

As a member of existing society the sage would marry and beget children, both for his own sake and for that of his country, on behalf of which, if it were good, he would be ready to suffer and die. Still he would look forward to a better time when, in Zeno's as in Plato's republic, the wise would have women and children in common, when the elders would love all the rising generation equally with parental fondness, and when marital jealousy would be no more.

As being essentially a social being, the sage was endowed not only with the graver political virtues, but also with the graces of life. He was sociable, tactful and stimulating, using conversation as a means for promoting good will and friendship; so far as might be, he was all things to all men, which made him fascinating and charming, insinuating and even wily; he know how to hit the point and to choose the right moment, yet with it all he was plain and unostentatious and simple and unaffected; in particular he never delighted in irony much less in sarcasm.

From the social characteristics of the sage we turn now to a side of his character which appears eminently anti-social. One of his most highly vaunted characteristics was his self-sufficingness. He was to be able to step out of a burning city, coming from the wreck not only of his fortunes, but of his friends and family, and to declare with a smile that he has lost nothing. All that he truly cared for was to be centered in himself. Only thus could he be sure that Fortune would not wrest it from him.

The apathy or passionlessness of the sage is another of his most salient features. The passions being, on Zeno's showing, not natural, but forms of disease, the sage, as being the perfect man, would of course be wholly free from them. They were so many disturbances of the even flow in which his bliss lay. The sage therefore would never be moved by a feeling of favour towards any one; he would never pardon a fault; he would never feel pity; he would never be prevailed upon by entreaty; he would never be stirred to anger.

As to the absence of pity in the sage, the Stoics themselves must have felt some difficulty there since we find Epictetus recommending his hearers to show grief out of sympathy for another, but to be careful not to feel it. The inexorability of the sage was a mere consequence of his calm reasonableness, which would lead him to take the right view from the first. Lastly, the sage would never be stirred to anger. For why should it stir his anger to see another in his ignorance injuring himself?

One more touch has yet to be added to the apathy of the sage. He was impervious to wonder. No miracle of nature could excite his astonishment--no mephitic caverns, which men deemed the mouths of hell, no deep-drawn ebb tides--the standing marvel of the Mediterranean dweller, no hot springs, no spouting jets of fire.

From the absence of passion it is but a step to the absence of error. So we pass now to the infallibility of the sage--a monstrous doctrine which was never broached in the schools before Zeno. The sage, it was maintained, held no opinions, he never repented of his conduct, he was never deceived in anything. Between the daylight of knowledge and darkness of nescience Plato had interposed the twilight of opinion wherein men walked for the most part. Not so however the Stoic sage. Of him it might be said, as Charles Lamb said of the Scotchman with whom he so imperfectly sympathized: "His understanding is always at its meridian--you never see the first dawn, the early streaks." He has no falterings of self suspicion. Surmises, guesses, misgivings, half intuitions, semiconsciousness, partial illuminations, dim instincts, embryo conceptions, have no place in his brain or vocabulary. The twilight of dubiety never falls upon him. Opinion, whether in the form of an ungripped assent, or a weak supposition, was alien from the mental disposition of the serious man. With him there was no hasty or premature assent of the understanding, no forgetfulness, no distrust. He never allowed himself to be overreached or deluded, never had need of an arbiter, never was out in his reckoning nor put out by another. No urbane man ever wandered from his way, or missed his mark, or saw wrong, or heard amiss, or erred in any of his senses; he never conjectured nor thought of a better thing, for the one was a form of imperfect assent, and the other a sign of previous precipitancy. There was with him no change, no retraction, and no tripping. These things were for those whose dogmas could alter. After this it is almost superfluous for us to be assured that the sage never got drunk. Drunkenness, as Zeno pointed out, involved babbling, and of that the sage would never be guilty. He would not, however, altogether eschew banquets. Indeed, the Stoics recognized a virtue under the name of 'conviviality,' which consisted in the proper conduct of them. It was said of Chrysippus that his demeanor was always quiet, even if his gait were unsteady, so that his housekeeper declared that only his legs were drunk.

There were pleasantries even within the school on this subject of infallibility of the sage. Aristo of Chios, while seceding on some other matters, held fast to the dogma that the sage never opined. Whereupon Persaeus played a trick upon him. He made one of two twin brothers deposit a sum of money with him and the other call to reclaim it. The success of the trick however only went to establish that Aristo was not the sage, an admission which each of the Stoics seems to have been ready enough to make on his own part, as the responsibilities of the position were so fatiguing.

There remains one more leading characteristic of the sage, the most striking of them all, and the most important from the ethical point of view. This was his innocence or harmlessness. He would not harm others and was not to be harmed by them. For the Stoics believed with Socrates that it was not permissible by the divine law for a better man to be harmed by a worse. You could not harm the sage any more than you could harm the sunlight; he was in our world, but not of it. There was no possibility of evil for him, save in his own will, and that you could not touch. And as the sage was beyond harm, so also was he above insult. Men might disgrace themselves by their insolent attitude towards his mild majesty, but it was not in their power to disgrace him.

As the Stoics had their analogue to the tenet of final assurance, so had they also to that of sudden conversion. They held that a man might become a sage without being at first aware of it. The abruptness of the transition from folly to wisdom was in keeping with their principle that there was no medium between the two, but it was naturally a point which attracted the strictures of their opponents. That a man should be at one moment stupid and ignorant and unjust and intemperate, a slave and poor, and destitute, at the next a king, rich, and prosperous, temperate, and just, secure in his judgements and exempt from error, was a transformation, they declared, which smacked more of the fairy tales of the nursery than of the doctrines of a sober philosophy.

PHYSIC

We have now before us the main facts with regard to the Stoic view of man's nature, but we have yet to see in what setting they were put. What was the Stoic outlook upon the universe? The answer to this question is supplied by their Physic.

There were, according to the Stoics, two first principles of all things, the active and the passive. The passive was that unqualified being which is known as Matter. The active was the Logos, or reason in it, which is God. This, it was held, eternally pervades matter and creates all things. This dogma, laid down by Zeno, was repeated after him by the subsequent heads of the school.

There were then two first principles, but there were not two causes of things. The active principle alone was cause, the other was mere material for it to work on--inert, senseless, destitute in itself of all shape and qualities, but ready to assume any qualities or shape.

Matter was defined as that out of which anything is produced. The Prime Matter, or unqualified being, was eternal and did not admit of increase or decrease, but only of change. It was the substance or being of all things that are.

The Stoics, it will be observed, used the term "matter" with the same confusing ambiguity with which we use it ourselves, now for sensible objects which have shape and other qualities, now for the abstract conception of matter, which is devoid of all qualities.

Both these first principles, it must be understood, were conceived of as bodies, though without form, the one everywhere interpenetrating the other. To say that the passive principle, or matter, is a body comes easy to us, because of the familiar confusion adverted to above. But how could the active principle, or God, be conceived of as a body? The answer to this question may sound paradoxical. It is because God is a spirit. A spirit in its original sense meant air in motion. Now the active principle was not air, but it was something which bore an analogy to it--namely aether. Aether in motion might be called a 'spirit' as well as air in motion. It was in this sense that Chrysippus defined the thing that is, to be a spirit moving itself into and out of itself, or spirit moving itself to and fro.

From the two first principles which are ungenerated and indestructible must be distinguished the four elements which, though ultimate for us, yet were produced in the beginning by God and are destined some day to be reabsorbed into the divine nature. These with the Stoics were the same which had been accepted since Empedocles--namely earth, air, fire and water. The elements, like the two first principles were bodies; unlike them, they were declared to have shape as well as extension.

An element was defined as that out of which things at first come into being and into which they are at last resolved. In this relation did the four elements stand to all the compound bodies which the universe contained. The terms earth, air, fire and water had to be taken in a wide sense: earth meaning all that was of the nature of earth, air all that was of the nature of air and so on. Thus, in the human frame, the bones and sinews pertained to earth.

The four qualities of matter--hot, cold, moist and dry--were indicative of the presence of the four elements. Fire was the source of heat, air of cold, water of moisture, and earth of dryness. Between them, the four elements made up the unqualified being called Matter. All animals and other compound natures on earth had in them representatives of the four great physical constituents of the universe, but the moon, according to Chrysippus, consisted only of fire and air, while the sun was pure fire.

While all compound bodies were resolvable into the four elements, there were important differences among the elements, themselves. Two of them, fire and air, were light; the other two, water and earth, were heavy. By 'light' was meant that which tends away from its own centre, by 'heavy,' that which, tends towards it. The two light elements stood to the two heavy ones in much the same relation as the active to the passive principle generally. But further, fire had such a primary as entitles it, if the definition of element were pressed, to be considered alone worthy of the name. For the three other elements arose out of it and were to be again resolved into it.

We should obtain a wholly wrong impression of what Bishop Berkeley calls 'the philosophy of fire' if we set before our minds in this connection, the raging element whose strength is in destruction. Let us rather picture to ourselves as the type of fire the benign and beatific solar heat, the quickener and fosterer of all terrestrial life. For according to Zeno, there were two kinds of fire, the one destructive, the other what we may call 'constructive,' and which he called 'artistic'. This latter kind of fire, which was known as aether, was the substance of the heavenly bodies, as it was also of the soul of animals and of the 'nature' of plants. Chrysippus, following Heraclitus, taught that the elements passed into one another by a process of condensation and rarefaction. Fire first became solidified into air, then air into water and lastly water into earth. The process of dissolution took place in the reverse order, earth being rarefied into water, water into air, and air into fire. It is allowable to see in this old world doctrine an anticipation of the modern idea of different states of matter--the solid, the liquid, and the gaseous, with a fourth beyond the gaseous which science can still only guess at, and in which matter seems almost to merge into spirit.

Each of the four elements had its own abode in the universe. Outermost of all was the ethereal 'fire' which was divided into two spheres: first that of the fixed stars and next that of the planets. Below this lay the sphere of 'air', below this again that of 'water', and lowest or in other words, most central of all was the sphere of 'earth', the solid foundation of the whole structure. Water might be said to be above earth because nowhere was there water to be found without earth beneath it, but the surface of water was always equidistant from the centre, whereas earth had prominences which rose above water.

When we say that the Stoics regarded the universe as a plenum, the reader must understand by 'the universe' the Cosmos or ordered whole. Within this there was no emptiness owing to the pressure of the celestial upon the terrestrial sphere. But outside of this lay the infinite void without beginning, middle, or end. This occupied a very ambiguous position In their scheme. It was not being, for being was confined to body and yet it was there. It was in fact nothing, and that was why it was infinite. For as nothing cannot be bound to any thing, so neither can there be any bound to nothing. But while bodiless itself, it had the capacity to contain body, a fact which enabled it, despite its non-entity, to serve, as we shall see, a useful purpose.

Did the Stoics then regard the universe as finite or as infinite? In answering this question we must distinguish our terms, as they did. The All, they said, was infinite, but the Whole was finite. For the 'All' was the cosmos and the void, whereas the 'Whole' was the cosmos only. This distinction we may suppose to have originated with the later members of the school. For Appolodorus noted the ambiguity of the word 'All' as meaning, (1) the cosmos only, (2) cosmos + void

If then by the term "universe" we understand the cosmos, or ordered whole, we must say that the Stoics regarded the universe as finite. All being and all body, which was the same thing with being, had necessarily bounds, it was only not being, which was boundless.

Another distinction, due this time to Chrysippus himself, which the Stoics found it convenient to draw, was between the three words 'void,' 'place' and 'space'. Void was defined as 'the absence of body', place was that which was occupied by body, the term 'space' was reserved for that which was partly occupied and partly unoccupied. As there was no corner of the cosmos unfilled by body, space, it will be seen, was another name for the All. Place was compared to a vessel that was full, void to one that was empty, and space to the vast wine-cask, such as that in which Diogenes made his home, which was kept partly fully, but in which there was always room for more. The last comparison must of course not be pressed. For if space be a cask, it is one without top, bottom or sides.

But while the Stoics regarded our universe as an island of being in an ocean of void, they did not admit the possibility that other such islands might exist beyond our ken. The spectacle of the starry heavens, which presented itself nightly to their gaze in all the brilliancy of a southern sky--that was all there was of being, beyond that lay nothingness. Democritus or the Epicureans might dream of other worlds, but the Stoics contended for the unity of the cosmos as staunchly as the Mahometans for the unity of God, for with them the cosmos was God.

In shape they conceived of it as spherical, on the ground that the sphere was the perfect figure and was also the best adapted for motion. Not that the universe as a whole moved. The earth lay in its centre, spherical and motionless, and round it coursed the sun, moon, and planets, fixed each in its respective sphere as in so many concentric rings, while the outermost ring of all, which contained the fixed stars, wheeled round the rest with an inconceivable velocity.

The tendency of all things in the universe to the centre kept the earth fixed in the middle as being subject to an equal pressure on every side. The same cause also, according to Zeno, kept the universe itself at rest in the void. But in an infinite void, it could make no difference whether the whole were at rest or in motion. It may have been a desire to escape the notion of a migratory whole which led Zeno to broach the curious doctrine that the universe has no weight, as being composed of elements whereof two are heavy and two are light. Air and fire did indeed tend to the centre like everything else in the cosmos, but not till they had reached their natural home. Till then they were of an upward-growing nature. It appears then that the upward and downward tendencies of the elements were held to neutralise one another and to leave the universe devoid of weight.

The universe was the only thing which was perfect in itself, the one thing which was an end in itself. All other things were perfect indeed as parts, when considered with reference to the whole, but were none of them ends in themselves, unless man could be deemed so who was born to contemplate the universe and imitate its perfections. Thus, then, did the Stoics envisage the universe on its physical side--as one, finite, fixed in space, but revolving round its own centre, earth, beautiful beyond all things, and perfect as a whole.

But it was impossible for this order and beauty to exist without mind. The universe was pervaded by intelligence as man's body is pervaded by his soul. But as the human soul though everywhere present in the body is not present everywhere in the same degree, so it was with the world-soul. The human soul presents itself not only as intellect, but also in the lower manifestations of sense, growth, and cohesion. It is the soul which is the cause of the plant life, which displays itself more particularly in the nails and hair; it is the soul also which causes cohesion among the parts of the solid substances such as bones and sinews, that make up our frame. In the same way the world-soul displayed itself in rational beings as intellect, in the lower animals as mere souls, in plants as nature or growth, and in inorganic substances as 'holding' or cohesion. To this lowest stage add change, and you have growth or plant nature; super-add to this phantasy and impulse and you rise to the soul of irrational animals; at a yet higher stage you reach the rational and discursive intellect, which is peculiar to man among mortal natures.

We have spoken of soul as the cause of the plant life in our bodies, but plants were not admitted by the Stoics to be possessed of soul in the strict sense. What animated them was 'nature' or, as we have called it above, 'growth'. Nature, in this sense of the principle of growth, was defined by the Stoics as 'a constructive fire, proceeding in a regular way to production,' or 'a fiery spirit endowed with artistic skill'. That Nature was an artist needed no proof, since it was her handiwork that human art essayed to copy. But she was an artist who combined the useful with the pleasant, aiming at once at beauty and convenience. In the widest sense, Nature was another name for Providence, or the principle which held the universe together, but, as the term is now being employed, it stood for that degree of existence which is above cohesion and below soul. From this point of view, it was defined as "a cohesion subject to self originated change in accordance with seminal reasons effecting and maintaining its results in definite times, and reproducing in the offspring the characteristics of the parent". This sounds about as abstract as Herbert Spencer's definition of life, but it must be borne in mind that nature was all the time a 'spirit', and as such a body. It was a body of a less subtle essence than soul. Similarly, when the Stoics spoke of cohesion, they are not to be taken as referring to some abstract principle like attraction. 'Cohesions,' said Chrysippus, 'are nothing else than airs, for it is by these that bodies are held together, and of the individual qualities of things which are held together by cohesion, it is the air which is the compressing cause which in iron is called "hardness", in stone "thickness" and in solver "whiteness"'. Not only solidarity then, but also colours, which Zeno called 'the first schematisms' of matter were regarded as due to the mysterious agency of air. In fact, qualities in general were but blasts and tensions of the air, which gave form and figure to the inert matter underlying them.

As the man is in one sense the soul, in another the body, and in a third the union of both, so it was with the cosmos. The word was used in three senses-- (1) God (2) the arrangement of the stars, etc. (3) the combination of both.

The cosmos as identical with God was described as an individual made up of all being who is incorruptible and ungenerated, the fashioner of the ordered frame of the universe, who at certain periods of time absorbs all being into himself and again generates it from himself. Thus the cosmos on its external side was doomed to perish and the mode of its destruction was to be by fire, a doctrine which has been stamped upon the world's belief down to the present day. What was to bring about this consummation was the soul of the universe becoming too big for its body, which it would eventually swallow up altogether. In the efflagration, when everything went back to the primeval aether, the universe would be pure soul and alive equally through and through. In this subtle and attenuated state, it would require more room than before and so expand into the void, contracting again when another period of cosmic generation had set in. Hence the Stoic definition of the Void or Infinite as that into which the cosmos is resolved at the efflagration.

In this theory of the contraction of the universe out of an ethereal state and ultimate return to the same condition one sees a resemblance to the modern scientific hypothesis of the origin of our planetary system out of the solar nebula, and its predestined end in the same. Especially is this the case with the form in which the theory was held by Cleanthes, who pictured the heavenly bodies as hastening to their own destruction by dashing themselves, like so many gigantic moths, into the sun. Cleanthes however did not conceive mere mechanical force to be at work in this matter. The grand apotheosis of suicide which he foresaw was a voluntary act; for the heavenly bodies were Gods and were willing to lose their own in a larger life.

Thus all the deities except Zeus were mortal, or at all events, perishable. Gods, like men, were destined to have an end some day. They would melt in the great furnace of being as though they were made of wax or tin. Zeus then would be left alone with his own thoughts, or as the Stoics sometimes put it, Zeus would fall back upon Providence. For by Providence they meant the leading principle or mind of the whole, and by Zeus, as distinguished from Providence, this mind together with the cosmos, which was to it as body. In the efflagration the two would be fused into one in the single substance of aether. And then in the fulness of time there would be a restitution of all things. Everything would come round regularly again exactly as it had been before.

To us who have been taught to pant for progress, this seems a dreary prospect. But the Stoics were consistent Optimists, and did not ask for a change in what was best. They were content that the one drama of existence should enjoy a perpetual run without perhaps too nice a consideration for the actors. Death intermitted life, but did not end it. For the candle of life, which was extinguished now, would be kindled again hereafter. Being and not being came round in endless succession for all save him, into whom all being was resolved, and out of whom it emerged again, as from the vortex of some aeonian Maelstrom.

PHYSIC

CONCLUSION

When Socrates declared before his judges that "there is no evil to a good man either in life or after death, nor are his affairs neglected by the gods", he sounded the keynote of Stoicism, with its two main doctrines of virtue as the only good, and the government of the world by Providence. Let us weigh his words, lest we interpret them by the light of a comfortable modern piety. A great many things that are commonly called evil may and do happen to a good man in this life, and therefore presumably misfortunes may also overtake him in any other life that there may be. The only evil that can never befall him is vice, because that would be a contradiction in terms. Unless therefore Socrates was uttering idle words on the most solemn occasion of his life, he must be taken to have meant that there is no evil but vice, which implies that there is no good but virtue. Thus we are landed at once in the heart of the Stoic morality. To the question why, if there be a providence, so many evils happen to good men, Seneca unflinchingly replies: "No evil can happen to a good man, contraries do not mix." God has removed from the good all evil: because he has taken from them crimes and sins, bad thoughts and selfish designs and blind lust and grasping avarice. He has attended well to themselves, but he cannot be expected to look after their luggage: they relieve him of that care by being indifferent about it. This is the only form in which the doctrine of divine providence can be held consistently with the facts of life Again, when Socrates on the same occasion expressed his belief that it was not "permitted by the divine law for a better man to be harmed by a worse", he was asserting by implication the Stoic position. Neither Meletus nor Anytus could harm him, though they might have him killed or banished, or disfranchised. This passage of the Apology, in a condensed form, is adopted by Epictetus as one of the watchwords of Stoicism.

There is nothing more distinctive of Socrates than the doctrine that virtue is knowledge. Here too the Stoics followed him, ignoring all that Aristotle had done in showing the part played by the emotions and the will in virtue. Reason was with them a principle of action; with Aristotle it was a principle that guided action, but the motive power had to come from elsewhere. Socrates must even be held responsible for the Stoic paradox of the madness of all ordinary folk.

The Stoics did not owe much to the Peripatetics. There was too much balance about the master mind of Aristotle for their narrow intensity. His recognition of the value of the passions was to them an advocacy of disease in moderation: his admission of other elements besides virtue into the conception of happiness seemed to them to be a betrayal of the citadel, to say as he did that the exercise of virtue was the highest good was no merit in their eyes, unless it were added to the confession that there was none beside it. The Stoics tried to treat man as a being of pure reason. The Peripatetics would not shut their eyes to his mixed nature, and contended that the good of such a being must also be mixed, containing in it elements which had reference to the body and its environment. The goods of the soul indeed, they said, far outweighed those of body and estate, but still the latter had a right to be considered.

Though the Stoics were religious to the point of superstition, yet they did not invoke the terrors of theology to enforce the lesson of virtue. Plato does this even in the very work, the professed object of which is to prove the _intrinsic_ superiority of justice to injustice. But Chrysippus protested against Plato's procedure on this point, declaring that the talk about punishment by the gods was mere 'bugaboo'. By the Stoics indeed, no less than by the Epicureans, fear of the gods was discarded from philosophy. The Epicurean gods took no part in the affairs of men; the Stoic God was incapable of anger.

The absence of any appeal to rewards and punishments was a natural consequence of the central tenet of the Stoic morality: that virtue is in itself the most desirable of all things. Another corollary that flows with equal directness from the same principle is that is better to be than to seem virtuous. Those who are sincerely convinced that happiness is to be found in wealth or pleasure or power prefer the reality to the appearance of these goods; it must be the same with him who is sincerely convinced that happiness lies in virtue.

Despite the want of feeling in which the Stoics gloried, it is yet true to say that the humanity of their system constitutes one of its most just claims on our admiration. They were the first fully to recognise the worth of man as man; they heralded the reign of peace for which we are yet waiting; they proclaimed to the world the fatherhood of God and the brotherhood of man; they were convinced of the solidarity of mankind, and laid down that the interest of one must be subordinated to that of all. The word "philanthrop," though not unheard before their time, was brought into prominence by them as a name for a virtue among the virtues.

Aristotle's ideal state, like the Republic of Plato, is still an Hellenic city; Zeno was the first to dream of a republic which should embrace all mankind. In Plato's Republic all the material goods are contemptuously thrown to the lower classes, all the mental and spiritual reserved for the higher. In Aristotle's ideal the bulk of the population are mere conditions, not integral parts of the state. Aristotle's callous acceptance of the existing fact of slavery blinded his eyes to the wider outlook, which already in his time was beginning to be taken. His theories of the natural slave and of the natural nobility of the Greeks are mere attempts to justify practice. In the Ethics there is indeed a recognition of the rights of man, but it is faint and grudging. Aristotle there tells us that a slave, as a man, admits of justice, and therefore of friendship, but unfortunately it is not this

CONCLUSION

concession which is dominant in his system, but rather the reduction of a slave to a living tool by which it is immediately preceded. In another passage Aristotle points out that men, like other animals, have a natural affection for the members of their own species, a fact, he adds, which is best seen in travelling. This incipient humanitarianism seems to have been developed in a much more marked way by Aristotle's followers, but it is the Stoics who have won the glory of having initiated humanitarian sentiment.

Virtue, with the earlier Greek philosophers, was aristocratic and exclusive. Stoicism, like Christianity, threw it open to the meanest of mankind. In the kingdom of wisdom, as in the kingdom of Christ, there was neither barbarian, Scythian, bond, nor free. The only true freedom was to serve philosophy, or, which was the same thing, to serve God; and that could be done in any station in life. The sole condition of communion with gods and good men was the possession of a certain frame of mind, which might belong equally to a gentleman, to a freedman, or to a slave. In place of the arrogant assertion of the natural nobility of the Greeks, we now hear that a good mind is the true nobility. Birth is of no importance; all are sprung from the gods. "The door of virtue is shut to no man; it is open to all, admits all, invites all--free men, freedmen, slaves, kings and exiles. Its election is not of family or fortune; it is content with the bare man." Wherever there was a human being, there Stoicism saw a field for well doing. Its followers were always to have in their mouths and hearts the well-known line-- *Homo sum humani nihil a me allenum puto*

Closely connected with the humanitarianism of the Greeks is their cosmopolitanism.

Cosmopolitanism is a word which has contracted rather than expanded in meaning with the advance of time. We mean by it freedom from the shackles of nationality. The Stoics meant this and more. The city of which they claimed to be citizens was not merely this round world on which we dwell, but the universe at large with all the mighty life therein contained. In this city, the greatest of earth's cities--Rome, Ephesus or Alexandria, were but houses. To be exiled from one of them was only like changing your lodgings, and death but a removal from one quarter to another. The freemen of this city were all rational beings--sages on earth and the stars in heaven. Such an idea was thoroughly in keeping with the soaring genius of Stoicism. It was proclaimed by Zeno in his Republic, and after him by Chrysippus and his followers. It caught the imagination of alien writers as of the author of the Peripatetic _De Mundo_ who was possibly of Jewish origin and of Philo and St Paul who were certainly so. Cicero does not fail to make of it on behalf of the Stoics; Seneca revels in it; Epictetus employs it for edification and Maucus Aurelius finds solace in his heavenly citizenship for the cares of an earthly ruler--as Antoninus indeed his city is Rome, but as a man it is the universe.

The philosophy of an age cannot perhaps be inferred from its political conditions with that certainty which some writers assume; still there are cases in which the connection is obvious. On a wide view of the matter we may say that the opening up of the East by the arms of Alexander was the cause of the shifting of the philosophic standpoint from Hellenism to cosmopolitanism. If we reflect that the Cynic and Stoic teachers were mostly foreigners in Greece we shall find a very tangible reason for the change of view. Greece had done her work in educating the world and the world was beginning to make payment in kind. Those who had been branded as natural slaves were now giving laws to philosophy. The kingdom of wisdom was suffering violence at the hands of barbarians.

www.ingramcontent.com/pod-product-compliance
Lightning Source LLC
Chambersburg PA
CBHW031427040426
42444CB00006B/724